治癒詩話

HEALING WORDS & POEMS

治癒詩話

TOM FUNG

治癒詩話

Published by ARNICA PRESS

www.ArnicaPress.com

Copyright © 2021 Tom Fung

Photos by Shutterstock Images

ISBN: 978-1-955354-07-3

All rights reserved. No part of this book may be reproduced or transmitted in any form or by any means, electronic or mechanical, including photocopying, recording, or by any information storage and retrieval system, without the prior written permission from the Publisher.

治癒詩話

To all my Patients

治癒詩話

治癒詩話

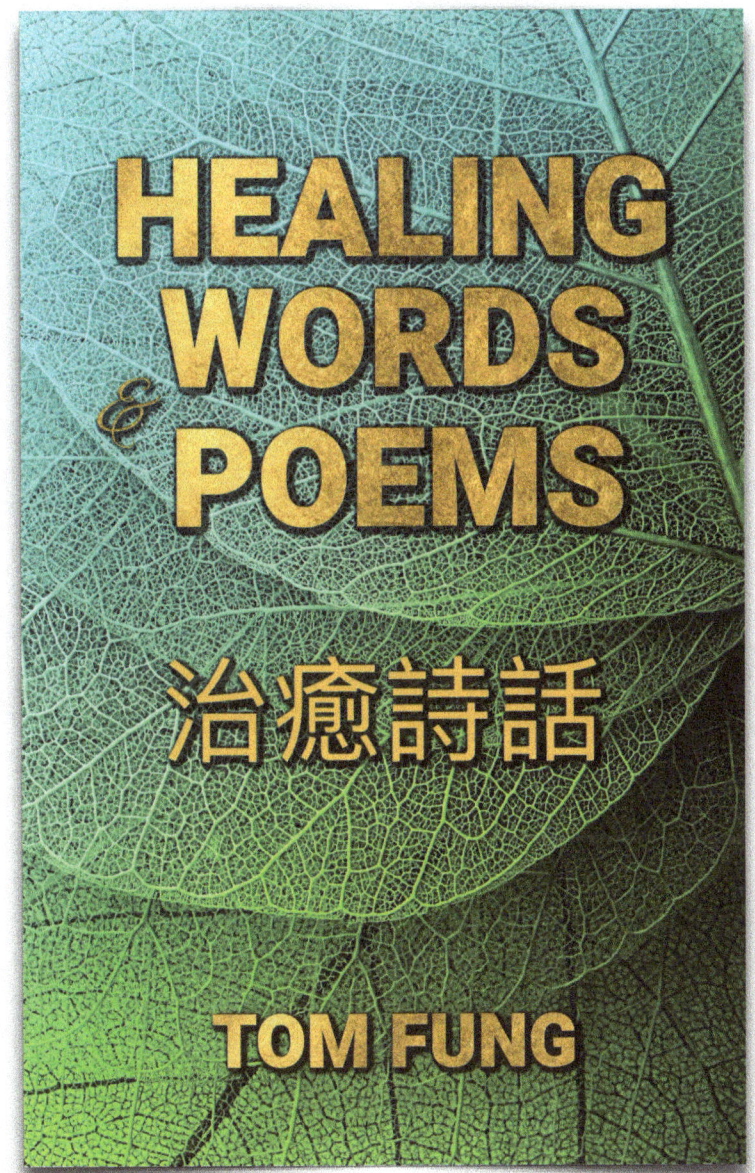

治癒詩話

治癒詩話

TABLE OF CONTENTS

Introduction..9

28 POEMS AND QUOTATIONS

1. Be 12
2. H.O.A.U 14
3. Hard and Easy 16
4. Modern Life 18
5. Discipline 20
6. People and Life 22
7. Realism 24
8. The 5 Recommendation & The 4 Achievements 26
9. Move Forward..28
10. Enlightenment 30
11. Climbing Mountains 32
12. Breathing...34
13. Enemy Tactics 36
14. Jealousy 38
15. Religious Conflicts 40
16. The Dialectical Method of Life 42
17. Interpersonal Relationship.............................44
18. Me, Me 46
19. Life Journey..48
20. The Wild pathway 50
21. Scandal 52
22. Blessed Christmas..54
23. Healing Journey 56
24. Steps to Success..58
25. The Next Life 60
26. Once You Gain it, don't Lose it......................62
27. A Mother's Love 64
28. A Poem for my Dearest Student....................66

About the Author..69

治癒詩話

治癒詩話

INTRODUCTION

I think the 21st century is a very different time in our history. We are challenged by the epidemic of Covid -19 and the 3 P's - Pollution, Population and Poverty. In addition, I strongly believe that many people are also affected by emotional problems with no clear direction in their life.

As an Earth citizen, everybody should contribute something to our world. This is one of the main reasons I would like to share my poems with the readers, who would like to gain some insight, learn to heal themselves and find a clear direction in life.

Since the early age of sixteen, I have been treating patients with acupuncture, Chinese herbal medicine, Chinese massage and meditations. Now, at the age of sixty-seven, I understand that many physical diseases stem from our unresolved emotional states. In Traditional Chinese medicine, they are named the internal Seven emotional factors. Since I am only a human with ten fingers, I can only personally heal a very limited number of patients. But my hope is that after readers explore this book, I might be able to help heal more people. Illness is a direct result and closely connected with our emotions. The mind, body and spirit are One.

治癒詩話

By reading my poems in this book, I am hopeful that you will discover a new way to heal yourself and find a some clarity with your life's direction and purpose.

Tom Fung

Aug 15, 2021.

Toronto Ontario Canada.

治癒詩話

POEMS AND QUOTATIONS

治癒詩話

BE

Be strong enough to face the world each day.

Understand your enemies.

Remain loyal to your friends.

Finish all the work before you go to sleep.

Stay wise enough to know you do not know everything.

Understand that everything requires team work.

Stay foolish enough to believe in miracles.

Be highly organized as usual.

是

治癒詩話

治癒詩話

H. O. A. U.

Illness may be caused by stress.

Stress is caused by disorganization.

Day to day highly organized people marry each other.

Calm your mind before you organize your mind.

Organize your mind when stress arrives.

Relax your mind and body before bedtime.

New life begins at sunrise

This is my key.

Highly organized as usual ~ h.o.a.u.

组织

治癒詩話

治癒詩話

HARD AND EASY

Every event is difficult in this world.
Things that are easy in the beginning,
will be usually difficult at the end,
and things that are difficult in the beginning,
will be usually easy in the end.

This is a natural phenomenon.
To be able to understand this concept,
we must put our whole body into it.

Constant talking and numerous theories
create an untrustworthy phenomenon.

Words and actions united,
serve to influence aspirations and credibility.

Face the event and return back to the event,
so your voice is heard and effective action follows.

Be honest with yourself
and calculate from an objective point of view,
then you will have a successful outcome of the event.

If you want to succeed in your endeavors,
you must follow a strategic course of action.

艰难而容易

治癒詩話

治癒詩話

MODERN LIFE

Advance with a steady step.
Get the big picture with a holistic concept.

Differentiate the essential from inessential.
Make an effort to accomplish one achievement a day.

The modern industrialized and commercialized society
presents great mental pressure with little physical movement!

So we must find a way to live based on the holistic concept.

Think about the bigger picture. Find the essentials.

First - emphasize health, second - knowledge, third - money.
One cannot rush achievement,
but rather, work overtime with longer hours.

Excessive stress can make a human lose their natural abilities.
Rushing can also cause mistakes.

Give up complications and be submissive to simplicity.
Make sure you have enough time to make an effort
for one accomplishment a day!

As an individual does well, more people will become well,
then the society will be well.

现代生活

治癒詩話

治癒詩話

DISCIPLINE

Discipline the body and cultivate the mind.

These are the ways to prevent illness.

Keep the body healthy and inspire aspiration.

These are the ways to success.

Peace and harmony are the laws of the Universe.

纪律

治癒詩話

治癒詩話

PEOPLE AND LIFE

Swim, swim, swim over the waves,
keep swimming to your destination.

Human life is difficult, but ever meaningful.

The sharp northern cold wind blows through my body,
but my heart is still as hot as fire.

The blood will flow till the last second.

Work for survival,
work for ideals,
and work for joy!

Human beings should be more than just objects.

A good relationship is delightful.

So let the energy flow naturally,
like the beautiful spring in nature
that reaches its level of ecstasy.

人和生活

治癒詩話

治癒詩話

REALISM

A person needs to have real knowledge and talent.

A high-rise building is built on the ground.

Foundation is the real answer.

There are not many shortcuts in the world.

Be honest with yourself and follow the right pathway.

One must not over-estimate their talent.

And for sure you mustn't fool yourself.

People's eyes are sharp.

Wisdom, knowledge and hard work all blend into one.

Yin and Yang must match morality.

现实主义

治癒詩話

治癒詩話

THE FIVE RECOMMENDATIONS

Avoid offensive thinking.

Avoid competitive thinking.

Respect other people's beliefs.

Try to maintain self-control.

Master Self-improvement through daily practice.

建议

THE FOUR ACHIEVEMENTS

Inner tranquility.

Harmony with the outside world.

Objective mindset.

Improvement of body, mind and spirit.

成就

治癒詩話

治癒詩話

MOVE FORWARD

Happiness is an inside job.

Action is better than empty talk.

Most diseases are formed by negative emotions.

Throw away and leave the negative situation!

The past is the past. Life is short.

Live for the present and plan for the future.

Courage is resistant to fear.

Find your way, my friend.

Move forward!

Peace and Harmony.

前进

治癒詩話

治癒詩話

ENLIGHTENMENT

Enlightenment is not easily acquired,
unless we pay the high price
through trials and tribulations.

The stone that we pick at random from the beach
is round in shape.

Nothing comes in a day – time is necessary for everything.

It is not easy to understand this,
but just as the constant lapping of water against the stone,
teaches us that the problems of life,
smooth themselves out with the passage of time,
so does the fine wine mellow with age!

觉悟

治癒詩話

治癒詩話

CLIMBING MOUNTAINS

Climbing one mountain after another,
personal ambition persists,
as indomitable as millions of mountains together.

No one is free of sorrows in life.

In fact, sweetness arises through affliction
and bitterness of sorrow.

Having the highest goal, yet lacking the wisdom is pointless!

Under fiercest circumstances, heroes remain calm and smile.

Whereas, little men panic,
hide in their beds and worry to death.

爬山

治癒詩話

治癒詩話

BREATHING

Breathe in the fresh.

Breathe out the stale.

Breathe in the future.

Breathe out the past.

Breathe in the vitality and breathe out the negative emotions.

Enjoy your life and air until your very end.

呼吸

治癒詩話

治癒詩話

ENEMY TACTICS

Staying in your territory
is the ultimate moderation.

Observe enemy's condition,
use calmness to control actions.

Injure the invader in a manner
without excessive action.

Yin and Yang must match the morality,
tactics are based on the situation.

Friends can turn to be your enemies;
and enemies can turn to be your friends.

敌人的战术

治癒詩話

治癒詩話

JEALOUSY

Jealousy is a dark and destructive force.

Jealousy is a sign of energy stagnation; it is a sign of disease.

Jealousy can cause a break down of one's personality.

If you focus your energy on your life,

the constructive energy will come.

Ha, ha, ha!

Sunshine will give you Direction.

妒忌

治癒詩話

治癒詩話

RELIGIOUS CONFLICTS

There are endless disputes because of religious conflicts.

There are endless wars because of religious problems.

There is endless bloodshed because of different beliefs.

When will our future children stop hurting each other?

When can we see the sunshine and breathe - in the fresh air?

宗教冲突

治癒詩話

治癒詩話

DIALECTICAL METHOD OF LIFE

General situation is based on holistic principles.

It is decisive when a rare phenomenon is individualistic.

Flexibility is based on a special situation.

Life and objects have similarities and dissimilarities.

整体原则

治癒詩話

治癒詩話

INTERPERSONAL RELATIONSHIP

One should always be lenient.
However, when dealing with little men,
one should be vigilant.

Peace and kindness are the main principles.

Use war to terminate war, use teaching to terminate war.

One should apply proper morals to others.

One should be faithful and just to friends
while remain tactical with enemies.

It is easy to make friends with people
at the same level or similar situation.

Vying with each other for benefits,
would only lead to destruction of both parties.

人际关系

治癒詩話

治癒詩話

ME, ME

I am the Sun and you are the other planets.

All of you people surround me.

My time is very important, but not yours, is this so?

Democracy works like a two way street!

Let us reset our minds.

Mutual respect is the key to human relationships.

我我

治癒詩話

治癒詩話

LIFE JOURNEY

Through Traditional Chinese Medicine,
we strive to alleviate the suffering
of those who endure illnesses.

Through Qigong meditation,
we learn to establish friendships
with legends from around the world.

Through visiting remarkable people and world wonders,
we inspire to spread knowledge and personal experience.

Through teaching the students,
we encourage to carry on past heritage,
and open up the future.

Through teaching morality,
we intend to ease the chaotic society.

Nevertheless, life is but an illusion,
it is comparable to the sudden changes in nature.

Just carry out your duties faithfully,
and fulfill all your obligations!

Take the last breath,
and disappear from the world.

人生旅程

治癒詩話

治癒詩話

THE WILD PATHWAY

As I enter into a wild pathway,
a breeze from a springtime evening
nourishes my internal organs.

The brook running endlessly,
harmonizes with the flow
of my inner bloodstream, as I stroll.

Trees of different sizes are everywhere,
I indeed experience my free spirit and a comfortable feeling.

Bird-song announces the arrival of spring,
and evokes the disruptive mouths of the little men!

As I pass mature trees that have dried up and tumbled down,
I lament for the deceased friends and relatives!

Eschew the branches of trees with thorns.

Eschew the envious little men.

As I travel my life's journey for the past forty-four years,
surfing the clear skies with beautiful sunsets,
I dismiss the stagnant energy, and free the spirit.

原野徑

治癒詩話

治癒詩話

SCANDAL

Scandalous behavior always has a motivation,
motive within motive can be a profound motivation.

Ordinary motive is caused by jealousy,
or when the mind is not calm, that is also a reason.

Hopefully my friend,
you don't believe in scandalous behavior,
for a scandal sometimes could be unreal.

The one who scandalizes is a little man,
the transcendent man does not believe in scandal.

A bright doctor understands the human mind the most;
when the mind is not calm,
it needs to be healed and cultivated.

The profound scandal is deeply political;
ordinary people don't understand that at all.

All incidents in our world are not stable,
the same principle applies,
that enemies and friends can be converted.

丑闻

治癒詩話

治癒詩話

BLESSED CHRISTMAS

I feel sorry for the lonely man who walks along by himself.

There is a lot of sadness before Christmas!

Modern society is complex, it carries a lot of pressure.

Self centeredness is dangerous.

Why has history brought us to this stage?

Where is our exit and our entrance?

The Sun falls in the West, and rises in the East.

The world rotates on its own.

祝福圣诞节

治癒詩話

治癒詩話

HEALING JOURNEY

A healing journey can be long or short.

To begin , find a skilled and honest healer.

Maintain a daily discipline.

Apply a holistic concept to healing yourself.

Practice a positive emotional state
to achieve the peace of mind.

You have to spend the money you need to spend.

No one can take their money to the grave.

Determination is the key.

Hopelessness hastens life's end.

疗愈之旅

治癒詩話

STEPS TO SUCCESS

Disciplining your body and cultivating your mind
are the ways to prevent illness.

Keeping the body healthy and inspiring aspiration
are the ways to success.

Peace and harmony are the laws of the Universe!

成功的步骤

治癒詩話

治癒詩話

THE NEXT LIFE

From the womb to beyond the tomb,

human life is but a dream.

Up and down, ebb and flow vicissitudes a precarious life.

Why did God not grant us an eternal life?

Towards the evening look at the sunset,

delay the time and wait for the sunrise.

下輩子

治癒詩話

治癒詩話

ONCE YOU GAIN IT, DON'T LOSE IT

Human life is short , and we only live once;
mistakes cannot be repeated all the time!

There are five essential things in life:
Wisdom, Health, Knowledge, Money and Opportunity.

WISDOM
Wisdom comes from tranquility,
Wisdom comes from experience. Wisdom comes with age!

HEALTH
Without health you'll go nowhere,
if you do not have good health,
gain it back by seeking a good health practitioner.

KNOWLEDGE
Knowledge is the road to success, it can protect you!

MONEY
Money is powerful.
It helps you save time and makes things easy.
Money can be dangerous, if we become a money - slave.
If you have no money you'll go nowhere!

OPPORTUNITY
When opportunity arises, take it, protect it and preserve it .

Above all, once you gain it, don't lose it!

不要失去它

治癒詩話

治癒詩話

A MOTHER'S LOVE

You brought up the children with great difficulty,
and your age is showing in the mirror.

A great mother is just like the vast Universe,
without you, history would stop.

Please put on your beautiful dress,
lets' listen to the wonderful music together.
Stay with me.

Breathe in the fresh air,
exercise your body and mind.

Lady, could you please dance with me?
Together we'll enter the tunnel of time,
and get back what we have lost.

Lighten up your heart with happiness,
diminish all the stagnant energy!

母亲的爱

治癒詩話

治癒詩話

A Poem
for my Dearest Student

A man who worked hard for his goals.

A man who although ill, did not surrender.

He constantly sought to improve himself.

An honest hardworking student, whom I will miss forever.

We had such good times during practice in my back yard.

You finally finished the last form before you died.

You left too early?
But someday we will enjoy this true art in the next world!

We are all looking forward to getting together with you again!

Good healers never die, they only fade away!

Your teacher and friend,
Tom

*Dr. Gerald Fujisawa passed away
on Dec. 11, 2009 at 9:15 PM*

给我的朋友

治癒詩話

治癒詩話

ABOUT THE AUTHOR
关于作者

Tom Fung is a Traditional Chinese Medicine practitioner and Acupuncturist practicing in Ontario, Canada. He is the eight-generation Master of Tai-chi mantis-style Chinese martial arts.

Tom was born in Shanghai, China on April 26, 1954. His childhood was challenging and the family moved to Hong Kong in 1957. His biological father spent more than twenty years in a hard labor camp, and Tom's mother was unwell, she suffered from mental illness. Tom always felt a deep compassion to help people, despite the fact that his life was challenging and filled with hardship. He worked very hard his entire life and observed how people live and behave.

Tom obtained a Diploma of Modern Chinese Medicine from the Chinese Medicine & Acupuncture Research Centre Hong Kong in 1976, and Diploma from the Canadian college of massage and Hydrotherapy in 1977. In March of 1976, Tom immigrated to Toronto, Canada, and became a Canadian citizen. He also traveled and lived in various cities in the USA.

治癒詩話

He established the Tom Fung Holistic Acupuncture Clinic in Toronto in 1979. He is also the Founder and Chief Instructor of Self-Balance Meditation Association, a master of Chen and Yang style Tai Chi and Qigong Meditation.

Tom has helped countless people from around the world that endured complex illnesses. He is of the opinion, that the human society suffers from numerous health ailments as a direct result of unhealthy emotional states and depression.

His desire is to share his poems and quotations with the readers who are eager to improve their overall state of well-being and consciously strive for self-improvement. In this book they will find valuable insight for their spiritual inner harmony and balance. The healing words and poems may also inspire those who need to improve their emotional states and seek peace of mind.

Tom Fung's degrees, Education & Licenses

- Obtained License of Reg. Traditional Chinese Medicine Practitioner in Ontario Canada in 2014
- Obtained License of Doctor of Oriental medicine & Acupuncture Physician from State of Florida USA in 2010
- Obtained Diplomate in Acupuncture of the National Certification Commission for Acupuncture & Oriental Medicine USA in 1994
- Obtained Diploma of Traditional China Internal medicine from the Xiamen University of China 1985.
- Obtained Certificate of Acupuncture & Moxibustion from the Xiamen University of China 1985

- Obtained Acupuncture License from the State of California USA in 1984
- Obtained Diploma from the Canadian college of massage and Hydrotherapy in 1977
- Obtained Certificate of Modern Chinese Medicine from the Chinese Medicine & Acupuncture Research Centre Hong Kong in 1976
- Obtained Diploma of Acupuncture form the Chinese Medicine & Acupuncture Research Centre Hong Kong in 1975

Tom Fung is a Freemason and a Shriner.

For more information visit his website at:
www.drtomfungclinic.ca

治癒詩話

www.ingramcontent.com/pod-product-compliance
Lightning Source LLC
Chambersburg PA
CBHW071413040426
42444CB00009B/2229